STUDENT

Ride On, Jesus

A BIBLE STUDY BASED ON AFRICAN AMERICAN SPIRITUALS

TAMARA E. LEWIS

Abingdon Press/Nashville

RIDE ON, JESUS: A BIBLE STUDY BASED ON AFRICAN AMERICAN
SPIRITUALS, STUDENT BOOK

Marilyn Thornton, Development Editor

Copyright 2004 by Abingdon Press

This book is printed on acid-free, elemental-chlorine-free paper.

Library of Congress Cataloging-in-Publication Data
ISBN 0-687-00759-3

All scripture quotations unless noted otherwise are taken from the New Revised Standard Version of the Bible, copyright 1989, Division of Christian Education of the National Council of the Churches of Christ in the United States of America. Used by permission. All rights reserved.

Table of Contents

 # Introduction

RIDE ON, JESUS: A BIBLE STUDY BASED ON AFRICAN AMERICAN SPIRITUALS continues a tradition started by Abingdon Press with *Plenty Good Room* (2002) and *Mary Had a Baby* (2003).

Why publish another study based on spirituals? According to historian John Lovell Jr., over 6,000 spirituals were created during slavery. Black people were not allowed much freedom of speech or movement. Yet through music, in particular, they found a way to communicate their hopes, joys, fears, and faith.

When the survival of a people is threatened, they find ways to record their history, their culture, and their beliefs about God. The Bible as we know it began to take its shape and form as the Hebrew children languished in slavery in Babylon. Unlike the Hebrews, who had a common language and whose captors, the Babylonians, taught them how to write and record in their own language (Daniel 1:3-4), Africans came from diverse tribes. Most were forbidden to learn to read and write any language whatsoever. However, God's Holy Spirit always finds a way to communicate to the people about God. God's Word does not return void unto God.

African American spirituals represent a unique form in sacred music. Through spirituals we have a firsthand record of some of the experiences of the African American slave. Through spirituals we know that slaves were sometimes motherless and fatherless and that in their homelessness they longed for a place to call home. The theology of spirituals gives clues as to their perception of a God of mercy, justice, and love in a world of cruelty, injustice, and racism. It is distinctly Afrocentric, reflecting ancient as well as newfound belief systems and functions.

While it is often said that those who do not know their history are doomed to repeat it, a Bible study drawn from spirituals is not just about looking back. To study spirituals is to draw on the faith and wisdom of those on whose shoulders we stand in order to grasp at a bright tomorrow. Spirituals are part of the heritage of African Americans, a birthright. God speaks to us from the music and poetry of these songs. Jacob desired the birthright of his brother who sold it to him for a pot of stew. By listening to and learning from the record left by enslaved black Americans, we show that we value, claim, and honor our birthright. We gain the opportunity to draw upon their strength as we face the challenges of the 21st century. By honoring our blessing, we acknowledge that which God has done; and we stand ready to receive that which God has in store for us. The whole world is in God's hand. "Eyes have not seen, nor ears have heard" how God will choose to bless the world through the gifts of the descendants of those who created African American spirituals.

Session One: Living in God's Care

Psalm 24:1; Psalm 104: 5-24

Key verse: "The earth is the LORD's and all that is in it, the world, and those who live in it" (Psalm 24:1).

Theme: Keep faith by showing love for self and all creation.

African proverb: The prosperity of the trees is the well-being of the birds.

"He's Got the Whole World in His Hands"

Chorus:
> He's got the whole world in his hands.
> He's got the whole world in his hands.
> He's got the whole world in his hands.
> He's got the whole world in his hands.

Verse:
> He's got the woods and the waters in his hands.
> He's got the woods and the waters in his hands.
> He's got the woods and the waters in his hands.
> He's got the whole world in his hands.

Verse:
> He's got the birds and the bees right in his hands.
> He's got the birds and the bees right in his hands.
> He's got the beasts of the fields in his hands.
> He's got the whole world in his hands.

Verse:
> He's got you and me right in his hands.
> He's got you and me right in his hands.
> He's got everybody in his hands.
> He's got the whole world in his hands.

Let's Listen: A Song of Assurance

"He's Got the Whole World in His Hands" is a positive, upbeat spiritual that contains a message of hope and joy. People of all ages and cultures enjoy singing this song of praise and worship. It can be found in many hymnals. The community joins in, reassured by words that emphasize the sovereignty of God. The melody is easy to learn in that it remains the same from chorus to verse. In the chorus, however, the melody and rhythm combine to create an emphasis on the word *whole*, reminding the singers that not some, not half, but the whole world is in God's hands. This includes the slave community out of which the song was created.

The words show a confidence by its creators in God's omnipotence, regardless of what appeared to be. It may have appeared that "Massa" owned everything they could see, yet the slaves knew that the earth was the Lord's. God was in control, and God was recognized as a good God. They may have been accused of stealing chickens even as their labor was being stolen from them every day. They realized, however that the birds and bees belonged to a God whose intention it was to provide for everyone. Even as their children were being sold away, slave parents hoped in a God who would take care of them wherever they were. Those children may have been lost to the parent, but they were not lost to God, because you and I and indeed the whole world are in the hands of God. In fact, the slaves knew God was a great God, the only God, who loved all people, all animals, and the earth itself with unconditional love. By the grace of God, the world had been created, the world was being sustained, and provisions were being made. Because of its message of faith and grace, "He's Got the Whole World in His Hands" is a song that has caught the imagination of people of many races, nationalities, and backgrounds to this day. It is a musical testimony of the goodness that springs from a Creator who loves us as dearly as a mother loves her children.

O Sing to the Lord

The spirituals of African Americans and the psalms of the Hebrew people have much in common. First, both forms are poetic. Poetry is utilized in all cultures as a way to provoke an emotional response, to probe the deeper meanings embedded in words and experiences.

Second, biblical psalms and the lyrics of spirituals speak to the particular experience of the people who produced them. The rhythms and word patterns accentuate implied and obvious meanings and elicit empathy, producing a shared environment with the creators and the current reader or listener. Many psalms and spirituals tell the story of how those who were being oppressed experienced the physical and spiritual deliverance of a God who cares. Psalm 105, for example, recounts in poetic form the entire Exodus story.

Additionally, psalms and spirituals express the awe of people being in relationship with a mighty Creator who is "mindful of them" and "made them a little lower than [the angels]" (Psalm 8:4, 5). Psalm 24, Psalm 104, and "He's Got the Whole World in His Hands" are excellent examples of how history, poetry, and awareness of relationship with God work together to produce abiding beauty, a witness to God at work in creation.

The World Belongs to God

The first verse of Psalm 24 boldly asserts that the world that God created continues to belong to God. It belongs to God who imagined it and fashioned it. There is no portion of creation that is not owned by God. Even as systems of oppression are perpetuated by humankind, all people and all creatures still belong to God.

In the system of American slavery, owners had complete control and oversight of their slaves, much like a person has complete control and oversight of an animal or even an inanimate object. From infancy, slaves were raised with the mentality of complete dependence and subjection to their masters, who ruled their lives with power and authority. Work, food, clothing, and human interaction were dictated and controlled by slave masters. If a slave wanted to marry and have children, he or she had to seek permission from the master. Yet, if a slave was designated as having to breed children in order to produce wealth for the master, deference to the master's desires had to be taken without question.

Slaves were sold away at the whim of masters; and legally, they had no recourse or influence whatsoever over their destiny or future. Their lives were relegated to absolute reliance on the master for livelihood, and this had a mental and emotional impact on the slaves. Masters taught their slaves that it would be impossible to live without their masters, who did everything for them. Slaves were encouraged to remain docile, compliant, and even fearful of the control and power that masters had over their lives. Simply put, although perhaps not expressed in these terms, slaves were forced to perceive their human masters as gods.

Psalm 24, a psalm of David, is a simple reminder to human beings that although we may have stewardship and even dominion over the earth, the true owner of the lands and the seas, the forests and the mountains, the people and the animals, is almighty God. As they sang in community, the slaves were assured that only God is God. We, like they, are humbled to understand that God is the author and originator of everything in the world.

Psalm 24 was sung in the procession of ancient Israelites into the Temple at Jerusalem. Therefore, as the people entered the house dedicated to the praise and worship of God, they were to ring out praises to the authority of God. As did the Hebrews, many African American slaves knew that regardless of the self-exalted supremacy of men and women in the affairs of the world, God held true power and had complete control. God is the Creator and is continuously creating. God has set the foundations of the earth in so stable a manner that nothing the psalmist can imagine will shake them loose (104:5). Psalm 104 tells in poetic form the magnificence of a God who has ordered creation and continues to sustain it.

The World Is Sustained by God

Psalm 104 enumerates the ways in which God continues to care for creation. The God of the Bible not only set the earth into being, but God continues to sustain it and provide for it. This psalm also shows how God has placed certain ecological balances in place. There is a holy interdependence, an environmental economy established by God over which human beings have "dominion" or responsibility (8:6). God causes grass to grow so that animals can be fed. God created plants for humankind to cultivate and have food. It is humankind's great privilege to participate in creation with God. Hunger, malnutrition, and famine are not part of God's economy for the world.

The word *economy* is derived from the Greek word *oikonomos*, meaning "one who manages the household." God created a world and set in place a way by which everything was to be managed, a system by which all creation would be provided for. God makes the "springs gush forth" so that every wild animal will have something to drink (104:10-11). God creates plants for animals to eat and for humankind to cultivate. God makes the trees strong so that birds may live and be safe. The diversity of God's creation produces different needs. Goats prefer high mountains (verse 18). Lions hunt for their food at night (verse 21). "O LORD, how manifold are your works! / In wisdom you have made them all" (verse 24).

Only God could organize creation in such a way that the death of leaves would mean the life of a tree. All summer long we enjoy green leaves on the trees. The leaves are nourished with food by the sun. This process is called *photosynthesis*. As the leaves take in carbon dioxide, they give off oxygen, which animals and humans need in order to breathe. As the year continues, the leaves die a brilliantly colorful death. They fall apart in a process called *decomposition*. The decomposed leaves become soil with rich nutrients that feed the other plants, including trees. The whole world is in the hands of God.

The Earth Still Belongs to God

It is God's wisdom and grace that creates, provides for, and sustains the earth, often in spite of the abuse of human beings towards plant, animal, and human life. American slavery represented a great abuse of human resources. Unfortunately, human beings continue to abuse one another economically, mentally, spiritually, and physically all over the world. Humankind also has great influence over nature. The industrialization and technological advances made over the past 300 years have increased a dependence on natural resources and produced a consumption that ravages God's beautiful earth. Resources that took thousands and thousands of years to develop are being depleted at an alarming rate. Wars are being fought and the labor of people continues to be exploited in order to support the lavish lifestyles of a few. The global economy does not benefit all on the globe.

In this generation, we have witnessed the extinction of rare plants and animals, the depletion of the ozone layer, and the shrinking of rain forests. Although we have been designated as stewards of God's creation, most agree that humankind has not been extremely resourceful or responsible in managing this household for which God gave responsibility. Waste, at local, economic, radioactive, and atomic levels threatens to not only eventually destroy human life but the planet as well. The time is now for all people to begin active participation in recycling campaigns, conservation measures, and the global push for kinder, gentler, methods of utilizing the earth's resources.

Like our ancestors who recycled clothing to make warm quilts, we must find economic means by which to keep the household. We must strive to remember that this is God's world, that all of humankind has been created in the image of God: "The earth is full of [God's] creatures"(104:24).

I Will Sing Praise to My God While I Have Being
(Psalm 104:33)

Part of our continuing song to God is in what we do as much as what we sing. Can we sing to the Creator God as we participate in destroying creation? Can we claim a status just a little lower than the angels when we debilitate our bodies with too much sugar, meat, drugs, and alcohol and too little exercise? Can we proclaim that the earth is the Lord's as we allow litter to pile up in our neighborhoods? Can we praise God for the trees while we refuse to use paper made out of recycled materials, knowing that new trees are cut down for virgin paper?

What do we say about the justice of God's economic structure when we turn a blind eye as dumps, landfills, and drugs overwhelm poor and ethnic communities? "The earth is the LORD's and all that is in it, / the world, and those who live in it; . . . / Who shall ascend the hill of the LORD? . . . Those who have clean hands and pure hearts" (Psalm 24:1, 3, 4).

In spite of their situation, believers in the slave community could ascend the hill of God with a pure desire for an authentic relationship with God. In their hearts they knew that slavery was not the sin of the slave. Let us honor them and the God of our salvation by finding ways to diminish the abuse of the resources God has so graciously given.

Food for Thought

1. What does "He's Got the Whole World in His Hands" tell you about the faith of the slave community out of which it sprang? Are you able to find and create beauty even in the midst of trouble?

2. What phrases in the Psalms help you understand the relationship between God and creation and the relationship between the rest of creation and humankind?

3. How can you help your church and community develop a sense of environmental consciousness?

Session Two: Keep Praying to God

Daniel 6:16-23

Key verse: "O, Daniel, servant of the living God, has your God, whom you faithfully serve been able to deliver you from the lions?" (Daniel 6:20b).

Theme: Raise hope by hearing that God answers prayer.

African proverb: Unless you call out, who will open the door?

"Daniel, Servant of the Lord"

Chorus:
> And the king cried, O Daniel, Daniel.
> O Daniel, Daniel.
> O that Hebrew, Daniel, servant of the Lord.

Verse:
> Among the Hebrew nation, one Hebrew, Daniel, was found.
> They put him in-a de lions' den. He stayed there all night long.
> And the king cried . . . (chorus)

Verse:
> Now the king, his sleep was troubled; and early in the morning he rose.
> How God had sent-a the angel down to the lock de lions' mouth.
> And the king cried . . .(chorus)

Let's Listen: A Song of Deliverance

"Daniel, Servant of the Lord" tells the miraculous story of Daniel in the lion's den. God's invincibility against the oppressive forces designed by human beings as portrayed in this story must have resonated deeply with the slaves. Out of a sense of justice and deliverance, they brought forth a song that in a few words explicitly describes the story of Daniel and his battle with evil.

The rhythmic quality of the song is steady and regular, and one can imagine slaves singing this song to the rhythm of their work in the fields picking cotton, tobacco, corn, or rice. As they sang, the slaves were reminded of the reward that comes through faith, prayer, and integrity. This song of deliverance sustained them, surrounded as they were by "patty-rollers" (patrollers), overseers, drivers (usually wielding a whip), "missuses" (mistresses), and "massas" (masters). Through the process of singing and working, the slaves became more deeply convicted in the ability and desire of God to deliver.

The song begins at the end of the story, plaintively echoing the king's cry, "O Daniel." However, rather than asking a question, the creators make a simple statement of fact that Daniel is a servant of the Lord. Through the repetition of his name, Daniel, the man is used as an example by which to live. Daniel's integrity is intact, his faith has been proven. "That Hebrew," of whom the king inquires, is faithful and true to the living God. "That Hebrew, Daniel," is a man who like them is oppressed, devalued, and surrounded by his enemies in a strange land. Nevertheless, he maintains his identity and is honored by the king and by God.

In only two verses the gist of the story is told. Daniel was found among the Hebrew nation. The originators of the song assume that those who sing will know what that means. They were in a place where many nations were living together; however, Daniel was among the despised Hebrews. In the 1960s, we might easily have sung "Among the Negro people, one Negro, Martin was found. / They put him in a Birmingham jail. / He stayed there all night long." Assign the chorus to President John Kennedy who sings, "O Martin, Martin, servant of the Lord," as he makes concerned phone calls inquiring about the well-being of Martin Luther King Jr., most likely assuring his safety upon having to spend several days in prison.

The first verse recounts how Daniel was put in the lions' den, a prison out of which no escape was expected. He remained there all night long. One night is a long time to spend in the midst of one's enemies. Indeed, one day in slavery was similar to a thousand midnights. From the time black people were pushed into the holding pens of Goree Island and onto cargo ships, prison has been a very dangerous place. Many black men have been known to go to jail and disappear.

The second verse tells how the king was disturbed and unable to sleep. In the morning, he discovered that Daniel was alive and unharmed. An angel sent by God had locked the lions' mouths. "O Daniel, Daniel, Servant of the Lord" reminds us of the rich storytelling tradition from which Africans in America came. In spite of the fact that most were not allowed to read about God, this spiritual lets us know that many in the slave community believed in a God that is able to deliver.

A Foreign Land

The first six chapters in the Book of Daniel are part of a genre that can be called conflict stories. They demonstrate how the oppressed Hebrews maintained cultural and spiritual integrity even as they lived in a foreign, hostile environment. Included in these chapters are the stories about Daniel and his friends choosing a diet that was different from the royal rations (1:3-21), the three Hebrew boys in the fiery furnace (Chapter 3), of King Nebuchadnezzar losing his mind (Chapter 4), and of the handwriting on the wall (Chapter 5).

These stories indicate that Daniel interacted with at least three different kings: Nebuchadnezzar, the Chaldean (Babylonian) king who destroyed Jerusalem and deported its royalty; Belshazzar, who lost the province of Babylon to the Persians and the Medes; and Darius, the Mede, who ruled Babylon upon the demise of the Babylonian Empire. Each story demonstrates that God reigns even in Babylon (present-day Iraq) and even when those who ordinarily would not have your best interest in mind are in charge.

The Persians and the Medes to the south (present-day Iran) had conquered the Babylonian empire. By his gifts and excellence, Daniel had risen to the top of the socio-political world of the Babylonian empire (6:1-3), yet he did not lose his witness concerning his own reality as a Hebrew. By the time Darius the Mede entered the picture, Daniel ranked third in power in the kingdom (5:29). Daniel continued to distinguish himself under the new government. Recognizing his gifts, Darius made plans to elevate Daniel in authority (6:3).

Praying to God

Without a doubt, Daniel's success in the Persian/Babylonian political system has already attracted great jealousy and hatred. Yet he did not lose his witness concerning his identity and faith as a Hebrew. He continued to serve God and pray. Daniel's devotion to the God of his ancestors is one more thing that set him apart. His enemies referred to him as "that Hebrew, Daniel" with a similar emphasis as sung in the spiritual. His Persian coworkers knew that the only way to get to him was by that which made him different, his ethnicity as demonstrated by his religion.

In those days, it was believed that each group of people had a god that supported and protected them. To pray to a god that was different from the one of the ruling class could be interpreted as treason. Daniel, however, was loyal to the king, a fact of which the king was aware. Daniel was just trying to do his job even as he practiced his religion. His Persian/Median coworkers devised a law that opposed the worship of any god other than the king. However, Daniel, faithful to the God of his ancestors, continued to worship the one true God.

In the story, Daniel's coworkers create a 30-day law that would work against any devout Hebrew. They appealed to the king's ego, "Whoever prays to anyone . . .except to you," in order to get the law passed. In prayer, one worships, petitions, and praises an entity believed to be omnipotent and worthy. The king was convinced that he should be treated as if he were God.

The law stipulated that persons found praying to anyone or anything besides the king had to be thrown into a den of lions. All the officials, including Daniel, were aware of the new law; but just as his enemies had hoped, Daniel continued to pray to the God of Israel. From the second floor of his house, by an open window that faced in the direction of Jerusalem, Daniel knelt to pray three times a day. He was true to his heritage even while surrounded by those who wished his downfall.

When his coworkers discovered him, they reported him to the king. Darius could not rescind his command even though he loved and respected Daniel. His own respect and authority were at stake. Daniel was thrown into the lions' den as the new law required. However, the king prayed that Daniel's God would deliver him.

Maintaining Cultural and Spiritual Integrity

Daniel prayed to God because he respected the authority of God over the authority of human beings. His faith was deepened the more he prayed, and such faith was able to sustain him even in the face of imminent danger. Early Christians had to face lions' jaws in Roman arenas as public spectacles due to their faith in the living God. They refused to acknowledge Caesar as a god, becoming martyrs as they paid the ultimate penalty for their faith. Indeed, unlike Daniel, most were not delivered from certain death at the clutches of the lions; but their steadfast faith in the midst of such horrors stood as an effective witness of faith to others. Through their testimony, the church was built and sustained.

African Americans also have found themselves surrounded by those who would eat them alive. Richard Allen, founder of the Free African Society and the African Methodist Episcopal

Church, was born in 1760, a slave in Philadelphia. His family was sold to another family in Delaware. By 1786, Allen had bought his freedom and become a Methodist preacher.

Church leaders of the St. George Methodist Church invited Allen to preach and minister to its black members. Allen had risen from a low position in society to one of respect and authority. This factor did not protect him from the lion of racism. By his preaching, the black membership of St. George increased dramatically. Their numbers threatened the sense of superiority of white members who decided to relegate blacks to certain areas of the church. Even as Allen knelt at the altar, praying (in the white area), the lions of impertinence, fear, prejudice, and racism surrounded him and demanded that he and his colleagues obey their law. Allen and others walked out and, maintaining cultural and spiritual integrity, proceeded to build institutions that testified of his pride as a black man and his faith in God.

Out of the Lions' Den

Like Daniel, African Americans have been brought out of the lions' den of chattel slavery. However, while slavery in America is no more, there are still forms of economic, educational, and cultural oppression that surround blacks as we seek to move forward in American society. There is the "glass ceiling" of the corporate structure and the culturally biased testing of the academic structure. African Americans continue to earn less for the same work accomplished in too many situations and be penalized for wearing hairstyles and clothing that indicate comfort with their cultural identity.

Black people driving in particular cars or on particular roads are stopped by police so often that the practice has inspired a new idiom. Instead of being DWI or Driving While Intoxicated, we are DWB, Driving While Black. Nevertheless, "We have come this far by faith, leaning on the Lord." Those who have been blessed to wear purple and gold (Daniel 5:29), to remain at the king's court (2:49b), and eat at the king's table (Chapter 1) must remember the example of Daniel and Richard Allen and never be ashamed that God created you black. Cultural identity is a gift from God and the God who gives all gifts answers all prayer.

God continues to open doors and shut lions' mouths. Upon hitting the glass ceiling, God can empower the creation of independent businesses that increase the wealth of the black community. Historically black universities like Howard, Fisk, Hampton, and Meharry continue to produce greater percentages of doctors, lawyers, and educators than majority institutions because of their commitment to the community. These institutions were founded on the prayers and faith of a newly liberated people who never failed to thank God for their deliverance. Like Daniel and our ancestors, may we keep praying to God.

Food for Thought

1. There is at least one other spiritual that uses the story of Daniel in the lions' den as its foundation. It asks the question, "Didn't my Lord deliver Daniel, and why not every man?" What is so compelling about this story for an oppressed community? The story has three components: integrity, persecution, and deliverance. Think for a moment and share a "lions' den story" with the group.

2. What is systemic racism? What are some other forms of oppression, subtle or overt, confronting people today? How can people of faith withstand and confront some of the contemporary " 'isms"?

3. What place do faith and prayer have in reducing or removing systems of oppression? How have you seen the power of God working in history as inspired by the faith of Christian people? Explain.

4. How does prayer help you in everyday life? Do you have a disciplined prayer life like Daniel?

Session Three: Acting on God's Will

Matthew 7:24-27

Key verse: "Everyone who hears these words of mine and acts on them will be like a wise man who built his house on rock" (Matthew 7:24).

Theme: Raise hope by seeing how wise action is rooted in God's will.

African Proverb: Words are spoken with their shells, but let the wise person come to open them.

"I Got a Home in-a Dat Rock"

I got a home in-a dat rock, don't you see?
I got a home in-a dat rock, don't you see?
Between the earth and sky, thought I heard my Savior cry.
I got a home in-a dat rock, don't you see?

Poor man Lazarus, poor as I, don't you see?
Poor man Lazarus, poor as I, don't you see?
Poor man Lazarus, poor as I, when he died he got a home
      on high.
He had a home in-a dat rock, don't you see?

Rich man Dives lived so well, don't you see?
Rich man Dives lived so well, don't you see?
Rich man Dives lived so well, when he died he got a home in
      hell.
He had no home in-a dat rock, don't you see?

God gave Noah de rainbow sign, don't you see?
God gave Noah de rainbow sign, don't you see?
God gave Noah de rainbow sign. No more water, but fire
      next time.
You better get a home in-a rock, don't you see?

Let's Listen: A Song of Warning

The musical and textual simplicity of "I Got a Home in-a Dat Rock" belies its radical message. The economy of words and notes expose an admonishment given by the slave community to all who would listen. In classic AABA form, the first two phrases are exactly the same in text. Melodically, the second phrase is also a repeat, only five steps up. That same music returns in the fourth and last phrase of the format.

The syncopated rhythm of the lead vocal part imitates a conversational tone. As the singer tells his neighbor, "I got a home in-a dat rock," he is simply giving a testimony, as the choral refrain provides an "amen corner" with "don't you see?" Each verse has the same melodic material, the same rhythm, the same refrain, and words that vary little within each strophe. Yet in four verses, the song moves from a clear statement of faith to a short interpretive story to a warning of apocalyptic* proportions. What genius!

In joyful tones the slaves declared, "I got a home in-a dat rock!" Even as their earthly homes were unstable and subject to change at the whim of a master's voice, the slaves who chose to believe in Jesus Christ were secure in a life anchored in a relationship with him. Despite their lack of literacy skills and book learning, they were wise because somewhere between the earth and the sky they had heard the voice of God and heeded their Savior's cry. The slaves understood that anchoring one's home in the rock was not just about hearing.

In this spiritual, they include the story about of "poor man Lazarus," identifying with one who is as "poor as I." With whom do they compare "rich man Dives"? The slaves were too shrewd to lay it all out, but certainly they were aware that living a life anchored in selfishness and grandiosity is the ultimate foolishness that will land you in hell. The humble life shared by Lazarus and the slaves will gain eternal life.

The slaves supported their understanding by admonishing their listeners with a warning drawn from the Hebrew Bible story about Noah. In a few words the slaves expressed an eschatological** hope. The present age will not last forever. Life in slavery will pass. The wise choice of building a home on the rock now will enable an escape from the fire to come.

*Referring to the apocalypse, a time of world destruction and the salvation of the righteous.
**Eschatology is the branch of theology concerned with the end times.

A Contradiction

Because of the close proximity that slaves had to their masters, they were able to observe and to compare living arrangements. Most slaves lived in poverty yet were exposed in full view to the lush and opulent living quarters of mansions and huge houses. They built, cleaned, and organized the beautiful homes in which their wealthy masters lived. They handled the delicate dishes and silverware, the costly decorations and furniture, the luxurious bed coverings and clothing. Slaves prepared mouth-watering meals for their masters and served those same meals in quiet refinement and service.

Yet, back in their own quarters, slaves were given the basest food to be eaten on the roughest plates with the meanest utensils. Sometimes they were even fed from a trough. Slaves wore tattered clothing, often made from potato and cotton sacks. House slaves may have received hand-me-downs. Most slaves wore shoes only in winter and clothing until it was beyond wear.

Food, clothing, and all supplies were tightly rationed. Slaves were well aware of their owners traveling in carriages: the ladies carrying intricate lace parasols to shield their skins from the heat, the men wearing shiny top hats and ornamented capes. Slaves, on the other hand, had no respite from the heat but were exposed to its glaring intensity from sunup to sundown. Most had no idea what it was like to ride in a carriage, although drivers were forced to carry the rich wherever they would like and attend to the horses, which often meant sleeping and eating in stables.

This apparent contradiction in the status of life was not only inequitable, it was a polar extremity. Yet masters and mistresses claimed to be Christians. Some may have even introduced a gospel of sorts to their slaves. Slaves had to make sense of this situation. They had to reconcile starvation, nakedness, poverty, and cruel work in the face of abundance and rest. Slaves, therefore, had to go to their God to get understanding regarding the sufferings of the have-nots in the face of the affluence of the haves. Only the light of Jesus' gospel could help.

A Master Storyteller

Jesus was a teacher and a storyteller. He taught through stories, riddles, and proverbs. With "I Got a Home in-a Dat Rock," African American slaves were inspired by Jesus' words from the Sermon on the Mount (Matthew 4:23-7:29) to include information from two other biblical stories (Genesis 9:12-17; Luke16:19-31) in order to emphasize the great truth of Matthew 7:21-28, that those who are wise will anchor their lives in the rock of Jesus Christ.

Matthew 7:13-29 is a series of warnings in which Jesus makes it plain that Christian discipline is one of deeds as well as words. Christian hope lies in dwelling in the faith. "But be doers of the word, and not merely hearers who deceive themselves (James 1:22)." He uses the images of wide and narrow gates and roads to indicate the choices that his listeners have.

The image of the wolf in sheep's clothing is placed beside fruit-bearing trees. The quality of the fruit will depend on how the tree is nurtured. Those who choose to listen to false teaching and be insincere in their relationship with God and humanity are deceiving themselves and producing bad fruit. They are like wolves in sheep's clothing. Jesus further warns his listeners that though people may fool themselves and others, God is not fooled by insincerity. True discipleship requires more than lip service. True discipleship requires action that is founded on the will of God.

After the warnings, Jesus tells a story about two men. One builds his house on rock. The other builds his house on sand. The house represents the life, the lifestyle, the place where a person dwells. The person who listens to Jesus and dwells in the lifestyle that Jesus teaches is building a house that can withstand crises of many kinds. This person is wise and is traveling the road that leads to life beyond the narrow gate.

The person who chooses the alternate route is building a house on sand. The foolishness of that person becomes evident at the slightest wind or rainfall. Sand slides away in the storm. That house will fall and the person dwelling therein will not enter into heaven. Jesus presents these two scenarios so that listeners could understand that they have a choice: sand or rock. The message is be smart and choose the rock.

Jesus Is the Rock

The stories and fables that were popular in the slave community characterized the triumph of the weak over the strong, the poor over the rich, and the simple over the wise. One has only to remember the triumphs of Br'er Rabbit over the fox and the wolf to know that this is true. Despite illiteracy and humble social circumstance, "I Got a Home in-a Dat Rock" reveals that many slaves understood that they were actually smarter than their masters. The wisdom of God not only gave them a hope for future justice, it enabled them to survive and even to thrive in a system designed to banish all hope.

The Word of God enabled the slaves to see beyond the insincere teachings of "slaves obey your masters" to an ability to seek true relationship with God. Slaves recognized the importance of building their houses of faith on the rock. Unlike their masters, most of whom concentrated on material wealth and worldly power, slaves held on to the rock of faith that would support them in the present and in the future. They knew that in their own lifetimes, rock-filled faith would comfort them when the storms of life hailed and railed against them. They found that by building a firm foundation on Jesus Christ, they could survive the deprivations they were experiencing with a sense of peace.

Slaves recognized that joy came not just from physical comforts or material possessions but in the abiding presence of God, who miraculously bestowed loving grace upon them in times of need. Such grace transcended the superficial comforts of material riches and fleeting pleasures. Singing "I Got a Home in-a Dat Rock" instilled in the slaves the reassuring conviction that only what they did for Christ would last.

Bling-bling

Solomon was right when he wrote, "There is nothing new under the sun" (Ecclesiastes 1:9b). In our day, extreme polarities continue in a global economy. It is estimated that 5 percent of the world's population consumes more than 80 percent of the world's resources. The rest of the world lives in poverty, with little access to health care, appropriate education, and modern living conditions. Mortality and life expectancy rates in developing countries reflect these deficiencies. The ascendancy of AIDS in Africa and Asia with limited access of medicines, information, and health care has lead to crises of epidemic proportions.

Today, extreme wealth can be found among persons of all races; and yet the same human tendency of selfishness as manifest in extravagance and opulence in the face of death and poverty has not abated. Rich governments, such as that of the United States, manage to designate only very small amounts of funding to help struggling economies and their helpless citizens.

A global message of materialism and worship of material things has clouded the judgments of most who are gifted with wealth to horde, display, and consume without a thought for the millions who literally starve to death each day. African Americans are just as guilty. Many a preacher has commented that black people buy what they want and beg for what they need. Black culture is responsible for yet another new idiom, "bling-bling," referring to the shiny things, material goods. Nevertheless, while African Americans as a "nation" have more income than many "third world" nations combined, black children in public schools still lag behind academically. Many neighborhoods that are primarily black do not thrive economically. Yet African Americans continue to consume material goods at extraordinary rates. Jesus' message of building one's home on rock must be re-taught to a new generation that has either not heard, or chosen to ignore, or forgotten the timeless warning that standing on the Word of God is not just lip service but action.

Food for Thought

1. How did the slaves interpret Jesus' message of building one's home on the rock in "I Got a Home in-a Dat Rock?" Explain.

2. How does Jesus' story in Matthew 7:21-27 and Luke 16:19-31 relate directly to "I Got a Home in-a Dat Rock?" How might slave masters, comfortable in their status and living conditions, have interpreted Jesus' message?

3. Describe your understanding and feelings about the distribution of wealth in the global economy.
   a. How do you reconcile the extreme polarities in the living conditions experienced by different people? Do you think it is justified?
   b. What are your opinions of the lifestyles of the so-called rich and famous? How do you think Jesus regards the lifestyles of such persons?

4. Are there any ways in which your life is built on sand? What can you do to adjust those areas in your life that seem to not be secure in the rock of faith and trust in the living God? What practical steps can you take to make changes?

Session Four: Following Jesus

Luke 9:57-62

Key verse: "Jesus said to him, 'No one who puts a hand to the plow and looks back is fit for the kingdom of God' "
(Luke 9:62).

Theme: Keep faith by knowing that a commitment to Jesus Christ leads to a place in God's kingdom.

African Proverb: The person who does not look ahead always remains behind.

"Hold On"

Chorus:
  Hold on, hold on; keep your hand on the plow, hold on.

Verse:
  Norah (Noah), Norah, let me come in;
   the doors are fastened and the winders pinned.
  Keep your hand on the plow, hold on, hold on.

  Norah said you done lost your track;
  you can't plow straight and keep a-lookin' back.
  Keep your hand on the plow, hold on, hold on.

Chorus:
  Hold on, hold on; keep your hand on the plow, hold on.

Verse:
  If you wanna get to heaven, let me tell you how. Just keep your hand on the gospel plow.
  Keep your hand on the plow, hold on, hold on.
  If that plow stays in your hand, land you straight in the Promised Land.
  Keep your hand on the plow, hold on, hold on.

Listening While Holding On

Jesus' admonition in Luke 9:62 that "no one who puts a hand to the plow and looks back is fit for the kingdom of God" provides an excellent metaphor for any person working with farm equipment. African American slaves toiling on plantations utilized this metaphor in the spiritual "Hold On." Through this song the community admonishes one another to stay committed: Keep your hand on the plow and hold on. As one plows up a row to be planted it will not do to allow the mule to have its own way. One must keep a firm hand on the plow if the rows are to be straight.

This spiritual is sung in a call and response format that stems from African song forms. A single individual leads the song while the congregation responds with a set refrain. The lead singer also introduces the new lines. One can imagine the community singing this spiritual as a work song, with the hoes being struck in rhythm with the humming. The underlying harmony is hummed in a simple but steady rhythm that may energize the work. The lead singer expends the most energy as his/her companions push on in agreement. Much of the singing done among the slaves was in unison with some improvisation. In "Hold On," the unison singing strengthens the encouraging message that upon hearing the good news and accepting the teachings of Jesus, they should not give up or give in no matter what.

Evangelization Among the Slaves

Many slave masters openly forbade their slaves to learn about the Christian faith. Some had simple reasons: The more time slaves spent in church or learning about faith, the less time they had to work in the fields. Other slave owners had more complex reasons. The legal issue of keeping baptized Christians in slavery had been solved as early as 1664 when colonies beginning with Maryland passed laws nullifying acceptance of Christianity as a mode to gaining freedom.

Black Christians began worshiping in church communities as early as 1725. Slave owners, however, continued to worry that slaves might grasp the message of freedom and liberation from the Bible. Learning the gospel of Jesus Christ might give slaves more self-esteem and self-awareness and make them dissatisfied with their status as slaves. They were correct to have this concern. Of the three most famous slave insurrections led by Gabriel Prosser in Richmond, Virginia (1800); Denmark Vesey in Charleston, South Carolina (1822); and Nat Turner in Southhampton, Virginia (1831), two—Prosser and Turner—were influenced by biblical imagery and story. Turner was considered to be a visionary and prophet in his community.

Often black slaves heard the same gospel as preached to whites in the camp meetings of the Second Great Awakening of the early 19th century, characterized by outdoor services of preaching and singing. In these egalitarian services, slave masters could not control the gospel. Slaves were able to catch on quickly and repeat these stories of faith and conviction. Slaves went on to hold their own secret prayer and worship meetings, raising their own songs of faith, sharing more Bible stories, and praying to God for adequate supplies and deliverance.

To stem the influence of the "invisible church" in which slaves met at night in tree groves and swamps, many denominations began to send missionaries into slave camps. These missionaries taught a version of the gospel similar to that which the slaves heard while sitting in the "colored" sections of the master's churches, that slavery was God's will for blacks and slaves should be obedient to their masters.

It is a testimony to the truth of the gospel that blacks were able to claim the Christian faith as their own. In the midst of their own situation, many were able to understand that Jesus came to liberate those who were in bondage and bind up the brokenhearted. In a life tightly circumscribed by the slave owner's law, the gospel gave the slave a means of controlling his or her own life. It gave them a set of ethics by which to live in the present as well as a hope for the future. They internalized the injunction to look forward in the faith, pressing on for the high mark of the calling of Christ Jesus. They strove to keep their hand to the plow, looking ahead, never back, towards spiritual and physical salvation and deliverance.

Following Jesus: Luke 9:57-62

Jesus' earthly ministry kept him traveling. As he and his disciples went from place to place, people claimed to want to follow him. One man told Jesus that he would follow him wherever he went. Jesus wanted to make sure that the man understood what it meant to follow Jesus. Even foxes have homes, and birds have nests; but he, as the one who is fully God and fully human, has nowhere to call home.

In order to truly follow Jesus, one must love God above home, family, and even life itself. God must be absolutely first. Jesus is asking, "Do you love me more than you love your home, your material comforts, your status in society? If so, you can follow me."

Jesus commands another man to follow him. This man replied that he first had responsibilities to his parents. He needed to care for them until they died, then he would be free to follow Jesus. Jesus' answer indicates that those who follow Jesus have new life and new responsibilities. Jesus had requirements for his followers. They should be available to preach the gospel no matter what else is going on in their lives. In Nigeria, among the Yoruba people there is a saying that "if it was good enough for our fathers, it is good enough for us."

Black Americans have a traditional gospel song that echoes this same sentiment.

Give me that old-time religion. (3x)
It's good enough for me.
It was good for my old mother. (3x)
It's good enough for me.

Jesus' answer indicates that those who would follow him should be ready to let go of traditions, old thoughts, and ideas. Sometimes we must bury traditions with those who taught them in order to look ahead to what God has in store.

As Jesus continues his journey, yet another man indicates that he wishes to follow Jesus. First, however, he needed to say goodbye to his family. Knowing the pull that family and familiar things can have on persons as they decide to make radical change in their lives, Jesus tells the man that he was looking back when he needed to look ahead. Using a metaphor that those living in farming communities could understand, Jesus reminded him that a person who is plowing a track cannot look back as he plows. Such action will yield a crooked row. The committed follower of Christ must always look ahead, never back, or they will fall off the path.

Slaves and Commitment

Christian slaves embraced the commitment to follow Jesus at all costs. Many had little to lose. They already lived a marginalized existence. They knew the reality of homelessness, having been torn from their homelands and placed in a society that would not allow them a sense of security in a new land. Homes and family were disrupted at will, yet slaves were expected to work with a sense of loyalty in every circumstance in which they found themselves.

The slaves could relate to Jesus. They were aliens with no place to lay their heads. While they would have to release some of the beliefs of their ancestors in order to claim citizenship in this new understanding of home, a commitment to Jesus Christ was an exercise in hope.

Similar to Jesus' audience, black slaves were familiar with farm culture and plowing. However, all the crops they would produce as slaves would belong to someone else. They had a hard row to hoe. As followers of Christ, they could take hold of his plow and gain the crop of a new community and a new sense of peace. By holding on to the faith, they were able to endure injustices of life and press on in spite of it all. They were able to make their lives the best they could be rather than give up in despair. They were able to sing new songs and lift up weary heads despite depressing conditions.

Staying Focused

How do we in modern western society relate to this admonition of focus and commitment given in Scripture and song? For many the plow is an antiquated image. Most people in our society are not farmers, and even farmers use more sophisticated farming equipment these days than a mule-drawn plow. However, we must remind ourselves of the nature of the plow—what the plow meant to Jesus' followers and what the plow meant to the slaves.

Keeping one's hand on the plow can be compared to driving a car. One must keep one's hand on the steering wheel. One must keep one's head forward and one's eyes on the road in order to avoid running off the road. While driving, one keeps looking forward and look backwards only for a glance to aid in forward movement.

There is much to distract in contemporary society. We often do not mind spending hours doing anything else except study the Word and worship God. Children and adults have limited attention spans produced by watching television, surfing the net, and playing video games. Yet following Jesus Christ requires focus and commitment. The twenty-first-century Christian must not think that the challenge is greater than any other generation. Can we really be more distracted than the slave who worked "from kin to cain't,"* never receiving the benefits of her or his labor?

By staying focused our ancestors gained our freedom. By staying focused we, too, will gain a brighter future for our children.

*"From kin to cain't" is the abbreviation of the expression "from kin see in the mo'nin' 'til cain't see at night," meaning that one worked from early morning as the sun came up until after the sun went down.

Food for Thought

1. In Matthew 9:57-62, do you think Jesus' listeners were ready to give up everything for him? Discuss the importance of placing Jesus first in our lives in order to be committed followers.

2. Many slaves who were exposed to Christianity refused to convert. What may have hindered them in accepting Christ?

3. "Hold On" may have helped slaves as they worked. Are there songs that help you in your daily walk? Choose one and tell how its message and music keep you going.

4. How can Christians walk the path of discipleship in today's society? What are some things that have distracted you in your Christian walk?

Session Five: Receiving the Holy Spirit

Acts 1:3-11; Revelation 19:11-16

Key verse: "But you will receive power when the Holy Spirit has come upon you; and you will be my witnesses" (Acts 1:8).

Theme: People will spread God's love by being witnesses for Jesus Christ.

African Proverb: Let your love be like misty rain, coming softly but flooding the river.

"Ride On, Jesus"

Chorus:
>   Oh, ride on, Jesus. Ride on, Jesus.
>   Ride on, conquering king.
>   I want to go to heaven in the morning.

Verses:
>   If you see my mother (sister, father, brother),
>   just tell her (him) for me,
>   I'm gonna ride my horse on the battlefield
>   'cause I want to go to heaven in the morning.

Listen: A Song of Justice

This spiritual acknowledges the kingship and lordship of Jesus Christ. It also demonstrates that the slaves understood that they were heirs in the Kingdom in that they had suffered with Christ in life.

With this musical arrangement one can imagine the day when Jesus returns with the presence of an angel choir and orchestra and the saints singing their praise to God. The opening line of the chorus is sung by a single voice. The melody ascends the chord like a triumphant bugle call. The other voices join as in a harmonic trumpet fanfare, echoing the same words, "Ride on, Jesus!" The angel choir joins in unison and agreement, "Ride on, conquering king." While the saints emphasize in rhythmic harmony, "I wanna go to HEA-ven in the morning!" this refrain is the ultimate desire of a follower of Jesus. It appears as a response to the call in the chorus and verses.

The words in the verses provide a witness concerning a reality of slave life. The song leader sings, "If you see my mother, just tell her for me." Many slaves had no idea where their mothers, fathers, sisters, and brothers were. Frederick Douglass reported that he remembered seeing his mother once when he was about five years old. He believed that children were removed from their mothers in order to interrupt the natural affection that mothers have for their children and vice versa.

The spiritual "Sometimes I Feel Like a Motherless Child" expresses the existence of many in slavery. Family members were sold apart in order to maintain control. Babies were sold for money so that mothers could work. Children were rendered motherless. These songs reveal that natural affections could not be eliminated. The longing for loving parents is only lessened by acceptance into a community of faith. Only with drugs like crack cocaine taken during pregnancy has it been found that the biochemical/emotional bonding that occurs between mother and child can truly be broken.

In 1826, even before she was legally free, Sojourner Truth,* with the help of Quakers, secured the return of her youngest child, Peter, who had been illegally sold to Alabama. Many in the white community could not understand all the fuss she was making over "a little nigger," but she was determined to have her child. From 1861-1865, Truth helped black mothers in Washington, DC, file suit for children stolen and sold into slavery in Maryland** where slavery was still legal.

The stories of the Bible stirred the imagination of African American slaves. When the leader sings, "I'm gonna ride my horse on the battlefield," she is letting the community know where she stands. She stands with Jesus. She has accepted him into her heart and is willing to be a witness for him. Jesus will own her, and she will get her white horse to ride on the battlefield with him in the days of glory.

Implicit in these statements is that heaven will include the opportunity to be rejoined with loved ones. Even as slave believers were marginalized and excluded in the church communities of their masters, the radical inclusiveness of the gospel message gave them the opportunity to imagine themselves and their family members as witnesses to and participants in a new world order. They created a theology that linked their own experiences with biblical stories and expressed that theology in song.

*Sojourner Truth (1797-1883), born Isabella Baumfree, was a slave in Ulster County, New York. New York abolished slavery in 1827.
**The Emancipation Proclamation abolished slavery in places that were in rebellion. Maryland did not secede. Slavery remained legal there until 1865.

Pie in the Sky?

Many spirituals can be interpreted as emphasizing heaven over earthly life as the only place where liberation could be achieved. Slaveholders encouraged slaves to accept their lot in life by asserting that their reward would come in heaven. Slaves certainly did aspire to the heavenly calling and looked forward to receiving the gift of eternal life. Often they had no choice but to develop hope out of what they perceived as immortality in life with Christ, a life in which all wrongs would be righted and all injustices put to rest.

This so-called "pie in the sky" theology was criticized by later generations because of its focus on the other life as opposed to pressing on for justice in the present. There was a call to lessen the emphasis on the other world and concentrate on the fight for liberation. Especially during the Civil Rights Movement, when people were actively pressing for equality in public facilities, schools, work places, and accommodations, the idea of sitting back and waiting for a reward after death was not appealing. Christians rightfully galvanized to mobilize for effective change that could be grasped in this life.

Still, the spiritual underpinnings of the message of hope during slavery were not abandoned. Certainly in light of the social and political strongholds that were in existence in their day, the only recourse that slaves had was to trust and to hope for a better life in another time and place. Yet, the focus of the slaves onto the grace and presence of the living God as transcending locality actually represented a universal quest to understand the meaning of life. Finding God over and above one's limited circumstances and futile quests for worldly fulfillment is an age-old endeavor in the history of humankind. Therefore, the slaves were tapping into the mystery of the questions of the whys, whats, and whos of human existence.

Enslaved believers understood that regardless of physical and worldly freedom, without spiritual and emotional enlightenment, one remains in chains. Their striving to seek God's kingdom through song, storytelling, and prayer, therefore, reflects the journey that all true Christians and God-seekers must take.

Jesus Ascends: Acts 1:8-11

Our lesson links two stories. One is about Jesus' ascension to heaven after declaring that his disciples would be witnesses for him in his physical absence. The other comes from John's vision of a conquering king riding on a white horse, which may be interpreted as Jesus' return from heaven.

In Acts, Luke chronicles Jesus' last meeting with his disciples. He promises that they will receive the power to witness to the world concerning his life and ministry. The disciples focused their attention on him. They saw as he was lifted up by the presence of God, as represented by a cloud. They watched the heavens until they could see him no more. They were no doubt mesmerized until two men in white robes appeared and told them to stop gazing. Jesus is alive, and he would part the clouds upon his return. The God of Abraham is a God of the living. Two heavenly beings informed the women at the tomb of Jesus' resurrection and it was perhaps these same two representatives that informed the disciples that Jesus' life would continue.

Jesus Returns: Revelation 19:11-16

Years later through a revelation, John becomes a witness to Jesus' return through the clouds. John sees the heavens open. A man on a white horse comes riding through. This man is called Faithful and True, The Word of God, the Kings of kings, and the Lord of lords! This man brings justice and truth. The rider of this horse is righteous. He has been crowned with many crowns and from his mouth comes a sword sharp enough to strike down anyone who stands in the way of the new world order. Who could this be but Jesus? Not only that, but there is a host of others clothed in white linen and riding on white horses. John describes them as armies. Those riding on horses are part of Jesus' entourage. They are with Jesus, the king.

The slave community could envision themselves riding on horses as part of the army of the Lord. Not only that, they encouraged one another to be witnesses for Jesus Christ. "Tell my relatives that I am a witness for Jesus. I'm on the battlefield riding a horse." The riders of the horses are wearing white.

The wearing of white cloth was significant in some African communities. It continues to be significant in many black churches. In black Methodist churches, communion stewardesses have a tradition of wearing white. In many other black churches, missionaries, church mothers, and deaconesses wear white for Communion and on special days. Additionally, very few slaves were allowed to ride horses. Riding on a horse would place their heads above the heads of the master. In the community of heaven, however, relatives can be found, horses can be ridden, and voices can be lifted. The first will be last and the last will be first. There will be a new world order as defined by the one who administers God's judgment. A new day was coming. Jesus was going to ride and so were they! They would be part of the justice that Jesus Christ would bring.

Justice and Peace

In the 1980's, when the Rev. Al Sharpton first became prominent as an advocate for justice, he and the crowds that followed him would lift their voices saying, "No justice, no peace!" As Christians in today's world, we know that no earthly comfort matches the joy and peace we will experience with God when we see Christ face to face. We also know that throughout this life, without the presence of Christ, our lives would be empty and meaningless. At the same time, we know that in his own lifetime Jesus was concerned about equity and justice in the daily lives of his people.

In the Luke 18, Jesus tells a story about how a woman, through her persistence, receives justice from an unjust judge. Matthew 25:31-46 reports that Jesus expects believers to be just and perform acts of mercy in order to be part of the new world order, the kingdom of heaven.

In our path of discipleship, we must pause to spend time with God in order to perceive a glimpse of the eternal. This is not escapism but grounding in the reality that we are part human and part divine. We gain strength for the battle when we feed all aspects of ourselves in order to be whole. Looking forward to our eternal home modifies our focus and behavior in this life.

We often feel helpless to help right any of the wrongs we see in society. Yet how can we be more helpless than Sojourner Truth? She was like the woman who had to approach the unjust judge. Jesus Christ is on the side of justice and peace. Jesus stands with us as we witness for him and for our fellow human beings, just as he will stand with us in the final judgment. We know that this life, this body, this form, is not the last word, is not the end. We strive to anticipate riding on with King Jesus into glory. Through our Lord, Jesus Christ, we can have justice and peace. Ride on, Jesus!

Food for Thought

1. Sojourner Truth apparently believed in justice, even as a slave. How can we corral our spiritual strength to fight for justice and peace?

2. What does it mean to ride with Jesus? What makes you a witness for Jesus Christ?

3. What are the requirements for entrance into the kingdom of heaven? Find Scripture to back up your answers.

4. What will it mean when Jesus comes again? How does the imagery of Jesus riding on a horse fit into your belief system? Where will you be when Jesus rides through the clouds?